TABLE OF CONTENTS

DISCLAIMER

The information presented in this book, "Beyond Masks: A Deep Dive into Personality Dynamics," is intended for general informational purposes only. The content within this book is based on research, personal experiences, and the author's interpretation of various personality theories. It is not intended as a substitute for professional advice, diagnosis, or treatment.

The author and publisher of this book have made every effort to ensure that the information provided is accurate and reliable at the time of publication. However, they do not assume and hereby disclaim any liability to any party for any loss, damage, or disruption caused by errors or omissions, whether such errors or omissions result from negligence, accident, or any other cause.

Readers are encouraged to consult appropriate professionals in the field for specific advice tailored to their individual situations. Any reliance you place on the information from this book is at your own risk.

The views and opinions expressed in this book are those of the author and do not necessarily reflect the official policy or position of any other individual, organisation, or company.

COPYRIGHT

BEYOND MASKS

A DEEP DIVE INTO PERSONALITY DYNAMICS

CLARISSA AUSTIN

BEHIND THE MASK

THE CONCEPT OF PERSONA

The concept of persona has deep roots in psychology and mythology, serving as a fundamental element in understanding human behaviour and identity. Derived from the Latin word for "mask," a persona represents the social face an individual presents to the world. This metaphorical mask is not merely a disguise but a complex interplay of roles, expectations, and self-perception.

Historical and Mythological Roots:

The origins of the persona can be traced back to ancient Greek and Roman theatre, where actors wore masks to portray different characters on stage. These masks allowed performers to embody various roles, often exaggerating emotions and characteristics for dramatic effect. Carl Jung, a prominent Swiss psychiatrist, later adopted the term to describe the social masks individuals wear in everyday life.
In mythology, gods and goddesses often assumed different personas to interact with mortals, highlighting the fluidity of identity and the adaptability required in various situations. The persona, in this context, becomes a tool for communication and connection with others.

Psychological Perspectives:

Jungian psychology delves into the persona as one of the archetypes, a collective unconscious element shared by humanity. According to Jung, the persona is a necessary social adaptation, enabling individuals to navigate societal expectations and norms. However, an overidentification with the persona can lead to a loss of authenticity and a disconnection from one's true self.
The persona is dynamic, changing across different social contexts. It encompasses roles at work, within family dynamics, and in various social circles. Understanding the persona involves recognizing the conscious and unconscious aspects of self-presentation, exploring how societal influences shape individual expressions.

Persona and Self-Identity:

The relationship between the persona and self-identity is intricate. While the persona serves as a social mask, it is not a complete fabrication. Instead, it reflects a curated aspect of the individual, shaped by cultural influences, societal expectations, and personal experiences. As individuals navigate life, they often tailor their personas to fit the demands of different situations, revealing the adaptability and malleability of the concept.

Challenges and Pitfalls:

Despite its adaptive nature, relying too heavily on the persona can lead to challenges. Overidentification with a particular mask may result in internal conflicts, as the authentic self struggles to align with the projected image. This discord can contribute to stress, anxiety, and a sense of disconnection.
Exploring the concept of persona involves a journey of self-discovery, acknowledging the masks worn, and understanding the motivations behind their adoption. Recognizing the persona as a tool for social interaction, rather than a complete representation of the self, opens avenues for authenticity and genuine connections.

In summary, the concept of persona encapsulates the intricate interplay between individual identity and societal expectations. By unravelling the layers of this metaphorical mask, individuals can embark on a journey toward authenticity, forging deeper connections with others and, most importantly, with themselves.

THE LAYERS WE HIDE BEHIND

The layers we hide behind constitute a multifaceted tapestry of identities, each carefully constructed to navigate the complexities of human interaction and societal expectations. These layers, akin to protective shields or masks, serve as coping mechanisms, self-presentation strategies, and tools for adaptation in diverse social contexts. In this exploration, we delve deeper into the psychological, sociocultural, and interpersonal aspects of the layers we consciously or unconsciously adopt.

Psychological Mechanisms:

At the core of the layers we hide behind are intricate psychological mechanisms shaped by a lifetime of experiences. Early childhood experiences, traumas, and societal conditioning contribute to the development of these layers. Defence mechanisms, such as denial, projection, and rationalisation, come into play as individuals strive to protect themselves from perceived threats. Understanding the psychological underpinnings of these layers requires an exploration of the unconscious mind and the intricate interplay of emotions and memories that shape self-perception.

Adaptive Nature of Layers:

The layers we construct are not static; they adapt to the ever-changing landscapes of our lives. In professional settings, individuals may adopt layers that project competence, authority, or conformity to organisational norms. In personal relationships, different layers may emerge to convey vulnerability, empathy, or a desire for connection. The adaptive nature of these layers is a testament to the human capacity for social navigation and the ability to tailor presentations of self to fit specific contexts.

Social Expectations and Conformity:

Societal norms and expectations play a pivotal role in shaping the layers we hide behind. From an early age, individuals are socialised to conform to cultural ideals and behavioural norms. This pressure to conform can lead to the creation of layers that align with societal expectations, even if they diverge from one's authentic self. The fear of judgement or rejection often drives individuals to adopt layers that mask their true beliefs, values, or unconventional aspects of their identity.

Emotional Layers:

Emotions, both expressed and concealed, contribute significantly to the layers individuals construct. Fear of vulnerability, shame, or the desire for acceptance can lead to the development of emotional layers. These layers serve as shields, protecting individuals from the potential emotional harm associated with revealing their true feelings or experiences. Unravelling the emotional layers involves a nuanced exploration of one's emotional landscape and the factors that influence the decision to reveal or conceal specific emotions.

The Dance of Authenticity and Adaptation:

Navigating the layers we hide behind involves striking a delicate balance between authenticity and adaptation. While the layers serve adaptive functions, an overreliance on them can lead to a sense of disconnection from one's true self. The dance of authenticity and adaptation requires self-awareness, introspection, and a conscious effort to align one's external presentation with internal authenticity. It is a dynamic process that evolves as individuals grow, learn, and engage with the world.

Peeling Back the Layers:

The journey towards authenticity entails a courageous exploration of the layers we have constructed. Peeling back these layers involves self-reflection, vulnerability, and a willingness to confront the discomfort associated with revealing one's true self. It is a process that requires self-acceptance, acknowledging imperfections, and embracing the authenticity that emerges when the protective layers are stripped away.
In summary, the layers we hide behind are intricate manifestations of psychological processes, societal influences, and emotional dynamics. Understanding and navigating these layers involve a nuanced exploration of the self, a commitment to authenticity, and a recognition of the interplay between adaptation and genuine self-expression. The layers, while serving essential functions, invite individuals to embark on a transformative journey towards a more authentic and interconnected existence.

EXPLORING THE PSYCHOLOGY OF MASKS

Delving into the psychology of masks unveils the intricate processes by which individuals navigate the complexities of self-presentation, societal expectations, and personal identity. The metaphorical masks we wear are not mere disguises; they are psychological constructs that serve various functions, both adaptive and protective. Understanding the psychology of masks involves an exploration of the subconscious mind, societal influences, and the interplay between authenticity and social conformity.

The Adaptive Function of Masks:

Masks, in a psychological context, are adaptive tools that individuals employ to negotiate the demands of different social situations. These masks allow for the expression of specific aspects of one's identity while concealing others. The adaptive function of masks is rooted in the human need for social connection and acceptance. By presenting a curated version of the self, individuals aim to fit into social norms, navigate relationships, and fulfil societal expectations.

Persona and Shadow:

Drawing from Jungian psychology, the concept of persona represents the social mask individuals wear in public. However, Jung also introduced the idea of the "shadow," which comprises the hidden, unconscious aspects of the self that are often suppressed or deemed socially unacceptable. The interplay between the persona and the shadow influences the creation of masks. Unconscious fears, desires, and unresolved issues contribute to the layers of masks individuals construct to manage the tension between societal expectations and authentic expression.

Social Cognitive Theory:

Albert Bandura's Social Cognitive Theory sheds light on how individuals learn behaviour through observation, imitation, and modelling. In the context of masks, individuals observe and internalise social roles and behaviours, leading to the adoption of specific masks that align with these learned patterns. The process is not merely imitation but an active engagement with the social environment, shaping the psychological landscape of self-presentation.

The Impact of Social Conditioning:

Social conditioning, stemming from cultural, familial, and societal influences, significantly shapes the psychology of masks. From childhood, individuals absorb societal norms, expectations, and cultural values that mould their self-concept. The pressure to conform to these ideals often leads to the construction of masks that align with external expectations, creating a delicate balance between fitting in and expressing one's authentic self.

Cognitive Dissonance and Authenticity:

The psychology of masks involves the phenomenon of cognitive dissonance, where individuals experience discomfort when their beliefs and behaviours are inconsistent. This discomfort may drive individuals to modify their masks to align more closely with their internal values or, conversely, to rationalise and justify the disparity between their authentic selves and external presentations. Exploring this cognitive dissonance unveils the intricate negotiation between authenticity and the desire for social acceptance.

The Unconscious and Symbolism:

Examining the psychology of masks necessitates an exploration of the unconscious mind and the symbolism embedded in these masks. Symbols carry potent meanings, often rooted in personal experiences, cultural contexts, or archetypal imagery. The choice of a specific mask may hold clues to an individual's inner world, desires, or struggles. Analysing these symbols provides insights into the deeper layers of the psyche.

Therapeutic Approaches to Unmasking:

Psychological therapies, such as psychoanalysis, cognitive-behavioural therapy, and humanistic approaches, often involve a process of unmasking. Therapists guide individuals in peeling back the layers, examining the motivations behind their masks, and fostering authenticity. The therapeutic journey explores the impact of masks on mental health, relationships, and overall well-being.

In conclusion, exploring the psychology of masks unveils a rich tapestry of adaptive strategies, societal influences, and unconscious dynamics. By unravelling the complexities of self-presentation, individuals gain a deeper understanding of their authentic selves, paving the way for personal growth, genuine connections, and a more conscious engagement with the world.

THE DANCE OF IDENTITIES

PERSONA VS. TRUE SELF

The interplay between persona and true self constitutes a fundamental dichotomy in the realm of human identity. Understanding this dynamic relationship involves a nuanced exploration of the conscious and unconscious aspects of self-presentation, delving into the layers individuals adopt to navigate social contexts while striving for authenticity and self-discovery.

Defining Persona:

The persona, as coined by Swiss psychiatrist Carl Jung, refers to the social mask individuals wear in various interactions. It is the outward-facing aspect of identity shaped by societal expectations, cultural influences, and the desire for acceptance. The persona is adaptive, allowing individuals to present themselves in ways that align with social norms and facilitate smoother interactions.

Unveiling the True Self:

In contrast to the persona, the true self represents the authentic core of an individual. It encompasses one's genuine thoughts, feelings, values, and aspirations, free from the influence of external expectations. The true self is not a static entity but a dynamic and evolving essence that requires self-awareness and introspection to uncover.

Persona as a Social Construct:

The persona serves a crucial social function, facilitating communication, cooperation, and connection with others. It is a means of navigating the complexities of social dynamics by presenting an adapted version of the self. However, the danger lies in overidentification with the persona, where individuals may lose touch with their authentic selves in the pursuit of societal approval or conformity.

The Tension Between Persona and True Self:

The tension between persona and true self arises from the constant negotiation between social adaptation and authenticity. Striking a balance between fulfilling societal expectations and honouring one's genuine identity is a delicate dance. Failure to manage this tension may lead to internal conflicts, a sense of disconnection, and the feeling of living a life inauthentic to one's core values.

Influence of Societal Expectations:

Societal expectations play a pivotal role in shaping the persona, often dictating acceptable norms, roles, and behaviours. The pressure to conform may lead individuals to construct personas that deviate from their true selves. This influence can be particularly pronounced in cultural, professional, or familial contexts, where adherence to specific roles is emphasised.

The Unmasking Process:

The journey toward authenticity involves an unmasking process – a conscious effort to peel away the layers of the persona and reveal the true self. This process requires self-reflection, introspection, and a willingness to confront uncomfortable truths. Unmasking is not about discarding the persona entirely but understanding its role as a tool for social interaction while allowing the true self to shine through.

Embracing Authenticity:

Embracing authenticity involves aligning one's actions, choices, and expressions with the true self. This alignment fosters a sense of congruence and integrity, enhancing overall well-being and mental health. Authentic living promotes genuine connections with others, as individuals engage in relationships from a place of honesty and vulnerability.

Therapeutic Approaches:

Therapeutic modalities, such as psychodynamic therapy, existential therapy, and mindfulness practices, often centre around the exploration of persona and true self. Therapists guide individuals in unravelling the layers, understanding the motivations behind the adopted personas, and fostering a deeper connection with the authentic self.

In summary, the dynamic interplay between persona and true self is an essential aspect of human identity. Navigating this dance involves a conscious exploration of self-presentation, societal influences, and the quest for authenticity. Striking a harmonious balance allows individuals to live more congruently, fostering a deeper connection with themselves and the world around them.

ADAPTING TO SOCIAL CONTEXTs

The human experience is inherently social, and our ability to adapt to different social contexts plays a pivotal role in navigating the intricacies of interpersonal relationships and societal dynamics. Adapting to social contexts involves a complex interplay of cognitive, emotional, and behavioural adjustments that individuals make to fit into diverse environments while maintaining a sense of authenticity and self-expression.

Cognitive Flexibility:

Adapting to social contexts requires cognitive flexibility – the ability to adjust one's thinking, perspectives, and behaviours based on the demands of a particular situation. This mental agility allows individuals to navigate diverse social settings, understanding and responding to varying expectations, norms, and communication styles.

Social Awareness:

A crucial element in adapting to social contexts is social awareness – an understanding of the social cues, norms, and expectations prevalent in a given environment. This awareness allows individuals to grasp the unspoken rules governing interactions, fostering a smoother integration into different social settings.

Role-playing and Social Roles:

In adapting to social contexts, individuals often engage in a form of role-playing, adopting specific social roles that align with the expectations of a particular situation. Whether at work, within a family, or among friends, individuals may seamlessly transition between roles, showcasing different facets of their identity to meet the demands of the moment.

Emotional Intelligence:

Emotional intelligence plays a significant role in adapting to social contexts. The ability to recognize and regulate one's emotions, as well as understand the emotions of others, enhances interpersonal dynamics. Emotional intelligence enables individuals to respond appropriately to the emotional tone of a social setting, fostering positive connections and effective communication.

Cultural Competence:

Adapting to social contexts becomes particularly nuanced in culturally diverse settings. Cultural competence involves not only an awareness of cultural differences but also the ability to navigate and respect diverse cultural norms, values, and communication styles. Developing cultural competence promotes effective cross-cultural interactions and mitigates the potential for misunderstandings.

Social Identity and Group Dynamics:

Individuals often adapt their behaviour based on their social identity and the dynamics of the groups they belong to. The social context within a family, a workplace, or a community can shape how individuals express themselves, emphasising the importance of fitting into group norms while balancing individual authenticity.

Communication Strategies:

Effective communication is a key component of adapting to social contexts. Individuals may tailor their communication styles, language choices, and nonverbal cues to align with the expectations of a particular setting. This adaptive communication enhances clarity and fosters understanding among diverse groups of people.

Maintaining Authenticity:

While adapting to social contexts is essential for successful navigation of diverse environments, maintaining authenticity within these adaptations is equally crucial. Striking a balance between fitting into a social context and expressing one's true self involves a conscious effort to align actions and behaviours with core values and beliefs.

Psychological Well-being:

Adapting to social contexts can significantly impact psychological well-being. Finding a harmonious balance between social adaptation and personal authenticity contributes to a sense of belonging, positive self-esteem, and overall life satisfaction. Conversely, an inability to adapt or the feeling of constant dissonance may lead to stress, anxiety, and a sense of social isolation.

The Evolving Nature of Adaptation:

Adapting to social contexts is not a static process; it evolves over time as individuals encounter new experiences, engage with different people, and navigate changing social landscapes. Embracing a growth mindset and a willingness to learn from diverse social interactions contribute to the continual development of adaptive skills.

In summary, the ability to adapt to social contexts is a multifaceted and dynamic aspect of human interaction. It involves cognitive flexibility, social awareness, emotional intelligence, and effective communication. Balancing adaptation with authenticity enhances interpersonal connections and contributes to the overall well-being of individuals in a social world.

UNVEILING THE COMPLEXITY OF IDENTITY

The concept of identity is a multifaceted and intricate tapestry, woven from the threads of personal experiences, cultural influences, social interactions, and individual self-perception. Unveiling the complexity of identity requires a nuanced exploration of the various dimensions that contribute to the formation and expression of who we are as individuals.

Layers of Identity:

Identity is not a monolithic construct but rather a layered phenomenon, akin to an intricate mosaic. These layers encompass aspects such as cultural identity, gender identity, religious identity, ethnic identity, and more. Each layer contributes unique colours and patterns, shaping the overall portrait of an individual. Unveiling the complexity involves acknowledging and understanding the interplay of these layers in shaping a person's sense of self.

Fluidity and Adaptability:

Identity is not static; it is dynamic and ever-evolving. The fluid nature of identity allows individuals to adapt to different life stages, environments, and experiences. The roles we assume in various social contexts, the changing dynamics of relationships, and the impact of life events all contribute to the fluidity of identity.

Cultural Influences:

Cultural identity plays a central role in shaping the complexity of one's sense of self. It encompasses shared values, traditions, language, and customs that are passed down through generations. Unveiling the cultural dimension of identity involves an exploration of how cultural influences contribute to one's beliefs, behaviours, and worldview.

Social Constructs and Norms:

Identity is often shaped by societal constructs and norms that define acceptable roles, behaviours, and expectations. Social norms influence how individuals perceive themselves and how they are perceived by others. Unveiling the impact of societal constructs on identity involves questioning and understanding the implicit and explicit expectations that shape our self-concept.

Self-Perception and Personal Narrative:

The way individuals perceive themselves and construct their personal narratives significantly contributes to the complexity of identity. The stories we tell ourselves about our past, present, and future create a narrative that informs our sense of identity. Unravelling this narrative involves exploring the stories we inherit, create, and internalise about who we are.

Intersectionality:

The concept of intersectionality recognizes that individuals embody multiple identities simultaneously, and these identities intersect in complex ways. Factors such as race, gender, sexuality, and socio-economic status intersect to create a unique and multidimensional identity. Unveiling the complexity involves acknowledging the intersections and understanding how they shape one's experiences and perspectives.

Identity and Self-Discovery:

Identity is not always fully known or understood. It is a continual process of self-discovery, self-reflection, and growth. Unveiling the complexity of identity involves embracing the ongoing journey of understanding oneself, acknowledging evolving facets of identity, and adapting to new discoveries about who we are.

Psychological Dimensions:

The psychological dimensions of identity delve into the inner workings of the mind, including self-concept, self-esteem, and the impact of psychological processes such as identity formation and identity crisis. Unveiling the psychological dimensions involves exploring the thoughts, beliefs, and emotions that contribute to how individuals perceive and define themselves.

Identity and Authenticity:

Unveiling the complexity of identity is closely tied to the pursuit of authenticity. Authentic identity involves aligning one's self-concept with one's genuine thoughts, feelings, and values. It requires self-acceptance and a willingness to embrace the richness and diversity within oneself.

In conclusion, unveiling the complexity of identity is a profound exploration that encompasses the layers, fluidity, cultural influences, social constructs, self-perception, intersectionality, psychological dimensions, and the ongoing process of self-discovery. Embracing the intricacies of identity allows individuals to cultivate a deeper understanding of themselves and fosters a more inclusive and empathetic appreciation for the diversity of human experience.

THE PSYCHOLOGY OF CONCEALMENT

INTRINSIC MOTIVATIONS FOR MASK-WEARING

The adoption of masks in various social contexts is a nuanced and complex phenomenon deeply rooted in psychological processes. While masks are often associated with concealment or protection, understanding the intrinsic motivations for mask-wearing unveils a spectrum of psychological, cultural, and individual factors that drive this behaviour.

Protection and Defense:

One intrinsic motivation for mask-wearing is rooted in the human instinct for self-preservation. Masks, whether physical or metaphorical, can serve as shields against external threats, be they physical, emotional, or psychological. Individuals may wear masks to guard themselves from judgement, criticism, or potential harm, creating a protective barrier around their true selves.

Identity Exploration and Expression:

Masks can provide a canvas for identity exploration and expression. Individuals may wear masks to experiment with different facets of their personalities, try on alternative roles, or temporarily adopt characteristics they find intriguing. This intrinsic motivation allows for a playful and creative exploration of the self within the safe confines of a chosen mask.

Social Harmony and Conformity:

Intrinsic motivations for mask-wearing often stem from the desire for social harmony and conformity. Individuals may don masks to align with group norms, societal expectations, or cultural traditions. This motivation reflects a fundamental human need for belonging and acceptance within a community, prompting individuals to adopt masks that resonate with prevailing social standards.

Coping Mechanism and Adaptation:

Masks can function as coping mechanisms, helping individuals navigate challenging situations or cope with internal struggles. In times of stress, anxiety, or uncertainty, people may wear masks to project composure, strength, or normalcy. This intrinsic motivation highlights the adaptive nature of mask-wearing as a tool for managing personal and social challenges.

Privacy and Boundary Setting:

Intrinsic motivations for mask-wearing may also revolve around the desire for privacy and the establishment of personal boundaries. Masks can act as a symbolic barrier, signalling to others the need for space or protection. This motivation reflects an individual's attempt to regulate social interactions and control the level of intimacy or exposure in different contexts.

Rituals and Symbolism:
Incorporating masks into rituals and symbolic ceremonies is another intrinsic motivation deeply rooted in cultural and psychological dimensions. Masks may be worn during ceremonies, rites of passage, or symbolic events to convey specific meanings, transitions, or transformations. This motivation emphasises the ceremonial and symbolic roles masks play in cultural and personal narratives.

Sense of Mystery and Intrigue:
Intrinsic motivations for mask-wearing can also include the allure of mystery and intrigue. Masks can evoke curiosity, capture attention, and create an enigmatic aura around the wearer. This motivation reflects a desire to engage others, provoke thought, or spark interest through the deliberate concealment of facial expressions or identity.

Empowerment and Anonymity:
Wearing a mask can empower individuals by providing a sense of anonymity. This intrinsic motivation allows people to express themselves or engage in activities without the fear of judgement or repercussions. The anonymity offered by masks may embolden individuals to step outside their usual comfort zones and explore aspects of their identity more freely.

Understanding the intrinsic motivations for mask-wearing unveils a rich and diverse landscape of human psychology. It underscores the complex interplay between individual desires, cultural influences, and the multifaceted nature of identity expression. As individuals navigate the intricate dance of intrinsic motivations, masks become powerful tools that shape personal narratives and contribute to the dynamic tapestry of human interaction.

THE IMPACT OF SOCIETY ON MASKS

Masks, both literal and metaphorical, are profoundly influenced by the socio-cultural tapestry in which they are woven. The impact of society on masks is a complex interplay of norms, expectations, traditions, and collective dynamics that shape the way individuals present themselves and navigate the social landscape. Examining this impact provides insights into how societal forces mould the psychology of mask-wearing.

Societal Norms and Expectations:
Societal norms and expectations play a pivotal role in dictating the types of masks individuals adopt. These norms vary across cultures, communities, and historical periods, influencing the acceptable behaviours, appearances, and roles deemed appropriate. The impact of societal norms creates a framework within which individuals craft their masks to align with prevailing expectations.

Cultural Influence and Traditions:
Cultural influence profoundly shapes the masks individuals wear, introducing unique symbols, rituals, and traditions associated with identity expression. The impact of culture extends to the symbolism embedded in masks, dictating the meanings attached to different types of masks and the occasions on which they are worn. Cultural norms become integral in determining the appropriateness and significance of mask-wearing.

Social Constructivism:
The concept of social constructivism emphasises how individuals derive meaning from their social environment. Society constructs narratives, categorizations, and classifications that influence the way individuals perceive themselves and others. The impact of social constructivism on masks is evident in the labels, roles, and expectations assigned to different identities, shaping the masks people choose to wear within these frameworks.

Socialisation and Peer Influence:
The process of socialisation, especially during formative years, deeply influences the masks individuals adopt. Peer influence, in particular, shapes the way people present themselves to fit into social groups. The impact of socialisation and peer dynamics can lead individuals to conform to certain stereotypes or adopt specific masks to gain acceptance and recognition within their peer circles.

Media and Pop Culture:

The media and popular culture wield significant influence over societal perceptions and trends, affecting the masks individuals choose to wear. Celebrities, influencers, and media representations often set standards of beauty, success, and identity. The impact of media can contribute to the adoption of specific personas or the emulation of popular masks depicted in mainstream culture.

Power Structures and Social Hierarchies:
The impact of societal power structures and social hierarchies is reflected in the masks individuals wear to navigate their positions within the social order. Masks may be adopted to conform to or challenge existing power dynamics, allowing individuals to assert themselves or blend into established structures. The impact of these structures influences the choices people make in presenting themselves to gain recognition or navigate societal expectations.

Political and Economic Influences:
Societal and political climates, as well as economic conditions, have a profound impact on the masks individuals choose to wear. During times of uncertainty or upheaval, individuals may adopt masks that project stability, resilience, or conformity. Economic factors can also shape the masks people wear, reflecting aspirations, social status, or responses to economic challenges.

Evolution of Societal Values:
As societal values evolve, so too do the masks individuals adopt. The impact of shifting values can be seen in the changing attitudes toward diversity, inclusivity, and personal expression. Masks become reflective of societal progress or resistance, serving as barometers for the prevailing values within a given cultural context.

Understanding the impact of society on masks underscores the dynamic and reciprocal relationship between individuals and their social environments. The masks people wear are not isolated expressions but are deeply entwined with the collective psyche, reflecting the ongoing negotiation between personal identity and societal expectations. The study of this impact provides a nuanced perspective on the intricate dance of identity within the broader context of human interaction.

UNMASKING PSYCHOLOGICAL PATTERNS

Peeling back the layers of the psychological masks individuals wear reveals a rich tapestry of patterns that influence thought processes, behaviours, and emotional responses. Unmasking psychological patterns involves a deep exploration of the intricacies that shape human cognition and behaviour, shedding light on both conscious and unconscious aspects of the mind.

Cognitive Patterns:
Cognitive patterns encompass the habitual ways individuals process information, make decisions, and interpret the world around them. Unmasking cognitive patterns involves identifying recurring thoughts, biases, and cognitive distortions that influence perception. Recognizing these patterns enables individuals to gain insight into their mental processes and make more informed and adaptive choices.

Emotional Patterns:
Emotional patterns pertain to the recurring emotional responses and reactions individuals exhibit in various situations. Unmasking emotional patterns involves understanding the origins of emotional triggers, habitual emotional responses, and the interplay between thoughts and emotions. By uncovering emotional patterns, individuals can develop emotional intelligence, fostering healthier and more resilient emotional states.

Behavioural Patterns:
Behavioural patterns refer to the consistent ways individuals act in response to internal and external stimuli. Unmasking behavioural patterns involves examining habits, routines, and automatic responses to different situations. Identifying these patterns allows individuals to assess the alignment between their behaviours and their goals, facilitating intentional and purposeful actions.

Defence Mechanisms:
Unmasking psychological patterns also involves exploring defence mechanisms employed by the mind to cope with stress, anxiety, or threats to self-esteem. Common defence mechanisms include denial, projection, and rationalisation. Understanding these defence mechanisms provides insights into how individuals protect themselves emotionally and navigate challenges.

Interpersonal Patterns:
Interpersonal patterns encompass the recurring ways individuals engage with others, form relationships, and navigate social dynamics. Unmasking interpersonal patterns

involves examining communication styles, attachment patterns, and relationship dynamics. Identifying these patterns facilitates more effective communication, deeper connections, and healthier relationships.

Coping Strategies:

In challenging situations, individuals often rely on coping strategies to manage stress and adversity. Unmasking psychological patterns related to coping strategies involves recognizing both adaptive and maladaptive ways of dealing with difficulties. Understanding these patterns empowers individuals to choose more effective coping mechanisms and build resilience.

Motivational Patterns:

Motivational patterns drive goal-setting, achievement, and personal growth. Unmasking these patterns involves exploring the underlying motivations that propel individuals forward. Whether driven by intrinsic or extrinsic factors, understanding motivational patterns provides clarity on personal aspirations and the factors influencing goal-directed behaviour.

Self-Perception and Identity Patterns:

Unmasking self-perception and identity patterns involves examining how individuals view themselves and construct their identity. These patterns are influenced by societal expectations, cultural influences, and personal experiences. Exploring self-perception and identity patterns facilitates a deeper understanding of one's authentic self and the layers of identity adopted over time.

Learning and Adaptation Patterns:

Learning and adaptation patterns encompass how individuals acquire new knowledge, skills, and behaviours over time. Unmasking these patterns involves recognizing preferred learning styles, approaches to problem-solving, and the ability to adapt to new circumstances. Understanding learning and adaptation patterns enhances cognitive flexibility and promotes continual growth.

Habitual Thought Loops:

Habitual thought loops represent recurring thought patterns that may be constructive or limiting. Unmasking these loops involves identifying persistent thought patterns that influence beliefs and attitudes. Breaking free from limiting thought loops allows individuals to challenge assumptions, broaden perspectives, and foster personal development.

In conclusion, unmasking psychological patterns is a transformative journey that requires self-awareness, introspection, and a commitment to personal growth. By unravelling these patterns, individuals gain deeper insights into their mental processes, emotional responses, and behavioural tendencies. This journey fosters greater self-understanding, resilience, and the capacity to navigate life's complexities with intention and authenticity.

MASKED EMOTIONS

EMOTIONAL EXPRESSION AND SUPPRESSION: THE DUAL NATURE OF MASKED EMOTION

In the intricate dance of masked emotion, individuals navigate a complex interplay between revealing and concealing their true feelings. Emotional expression and suppression, within the context of emotional masking, create a dual dynamic that reflects the delicate balance between authenticity and the societal expectations imposed by the emotional mask.

Unveiling Masked Emotional Expression:
Masked emotional expression involves the art of revealing selected emotions while concealing others. Individuals adept at emotional masking may strategically choose which feelings to display, aligning them with social norms and expectations. This nuanced expression allows for a controlled and curated presentation of emotions that serves specific social or personal objectives.

Cultural Appropriateness: The choice of which emotions to express may be influenced by cultural norms and appropriateness. Individuals may align their emotional expression with culturally accepted displays, showcasing emotions deemed suitable for a given context while concealing those that might be frowned upon.

Selective Emotional Displays: Masked emotional expression often entails selectively revealing emotions that align with the desired narrative or societal expectations. This can involve showcasing positivity, confidence, or composure while suppressing emotions perceived as vulnerable or socially undesirable.

Concealing Authentic Emotions:
Suppression of authentic emotions within the realm of masked emotion involves hiding genuine feelings behind a carefully constructed emotional façade. This intentional concealment may be driven by various factors, including the desire to avoid judgement, conform to social norms, or maintain a particular image.

Fear of Vulnerability: Individuals wearing emotional masks may fear the vulnerability associated with revealing authentic emotions. The fear of being judged or misunderstood may lead to the conscious suppression of genuine feelings, creating a protective shield against potential emotional exposure.

Social Image Maintenance: The need to maintain a specific social image or conform to societal expectations can drive the suppression of authentic emotions. Individuals may prioritise presenting an emotionally composed or positive front to align with perceived societal ideals.

Tension Between Authenticity and Conformity:
The dual nature of masked emotion introduces a tension between the authenticity of one's emotional experience and the conformity required by societal norms. Navigating this tension involves a constant negotiation between expressing genuine emotions and adhering to the expectations imposed by the emotional mask.

Strategic Balancing Act: Individuals engaged in masked emotion perform a strategic balancing act, determining when and how to authentically express emotions while adhering to societal norms. This delicate equilibrium requires a keen understanding of social contexts and a nuanced awareness of emotional cues.

Emotional Intelligence in Masked Emotion:
Emotional intelligence becomes a crucial factor in deciphering the intricacies of emotional expression and suppression within masked emotion. Individuals with high emotional intelligence can navigate the dual nature of masked emotion by discerning authentic emotional signals, understanding societal expectations, and making informed decisions about how to express or suppress emotions in a given context.

Impact on Mental Well-being:
The dual nature of masked emotion carries implications for mental well-being. Chronic misalignment between authentic emotions and expressed emotions, or persistent suppression of genuine feelings, can contribute to emotional dissonance, stress, and challenges in maintaining a healthy emotional state.

Strategies for Balancing Expression and Suppression:
Navigating the dual nature of masked emotion requires the development of strategies that balance authentic emotional expression with societal expectations. These strategies may include cultivating emotional self-awareness, creating safe spaces for genuine expression, and seeking support through trusted relationships or therapeutic interventions.

In conclusion, the exploration of emotional expression and suppression within the context of masked emotion reveals an intricate dance between authenticity and societal conformity. Unravelling this dual nature provides insights into the complex psychological processes that individuals engage in as they navigate the delicate balance between revealing and concealing their true emotional selves.

THE TOLL OF HIDDEN FEELINGS: UNMASKING THE IMPACT

In the realm of masked emotion, the hidden feelings concealed beneath emotional facades carry a significant toll, impacting various aspects of individuals' mental, emotional, and relational landscapes. Unmasking the toll of hidden feelings involves recognizing the profound implications of suppressing genuine emotions and the repercussions it poses on individual well-being.

Emotional Dissonance:
Hidden feelings create a discord between authentic emotions and the expressed ones. This emotional dissonance, born from the disparity between true feelings and those presented, can lead to inner conflict, confusion, and a sense of emotional incongruence. Over time, this dissonance may erode emotional authenticity and self-understanding.

Psychological Stress and Strain:
Suppressing genuine emotions exerts psychological stress and strain on individuals. The effort required to maintain emotional masks, coupled with the internal conflict of concealing authentic feelings, can lead to heightened stress levels, contributing to mental fatigue, and emotional exhaustion.

Impact on Mental Health:
The toll of hidden feelings extends to mental health repercussions. Chronic suppression of genuine emotions may lead to increased anxiety, depression, or other mental health challenges. The accumulation of unexpressed emotions can manifest as psychological distress, affecting overall mental well-being.

Inhibition of Authentic Connections:
Concealing genuine emotions inhibits the ability to form authentic connections. Masked emotion impedes genuine emotional expression and, in turn, hinders the development

of meaningful relationships. The inability to express true feelings may create barriers to intimacy and genuine connection with others.

Diminished Self-Awareness:

Continuous suppression of genuine emotions may lead to diminished self-awareness. Individuals may lose touch with their authentic emotional landscape, making it challenging to understand and process their feelings effectively. This lack of self-awareness can impede personal growth and emotional resilience.

Disrupted Emotional Regulation:

The toll of hidden feelings disrupts emotional regulation. Suppressed emotions may surface unexpectedly or inappropriately, leading to outbursts, mood swings, or difficulties in managing emotions. This disruption in emotional regulation can affect decision-making and interpersonal interactions.

Physical Health Ramifications:

The toll of hidden feelings can extend to physical health ramifications. Prolonged emotional suppression has been linked to increased stress-related physiological responses, potentially impacting immune function, cardiovascular health, and overall physical well-being.

Impact on Identity and Authenticity:

The toll of hidden feelings influences one's sense of identity and authenticity. Continuously wearing emotional masks may blur the lines between the true self and the presented self, leading to a sense of disconnection from one's genuine emotions and identity.

Long-term Relational Implications:

The toll of hidden feelings can have long-term implications on relationships. Difficulty in expressing genuine emotions may create distance or miscommunication in relationships, impacting trust, intimacy, and the ability to connect authentically.

In summary, the toll of hidden feelings within masked emotion encompasses multifaceted repercussions on individuals' mental, emotional, and relational well-being. Unmasking this toll involves acknowledging the profound impact of suppressing genuine emotions and underscores the importance of fostering emotional authenticity and creating spaces for genuine emotional expression to promote holistic well-being.

STRATEGIES FOR EMOTIONAL AUTHENTICITY: UNVEILING GENUINE EXPRESSION

In the intricate landscape of masked emotion, the pursuit of emotional authenticity becomes a transformative journey. Unmasking genuine expression involves adopting strategies that empower individuals to navigate the complexities of societal expectations, cultural influences, and internal dynamics while fostering a deeper connection with their authentic emotional selves.

Cultivating Emotional Self-Awareness:
The foundation for emotional authenticity lies in cultivating emotional self-awareness. Individuals can embark on a journey of self-discovery, engaging in reflective practices such as journaling, mindfulness, or therapy to explore and understand their genuine emotions. Developing a keen awareness of internal emotional landscapes enables a more authentic expression of feelings.

Creating Safe Spaces for Expression:
Establishing safe spaces for genuine emotional expression is essential within the realm of masked emotion. Whether through trusted relationships, support groups, or therapeutic settings, creating environments where individuals feel accepted and understood encourages the unmasking of true emotions without fear of judgement.

Practising Vulnerability:
Vulnerability is a powerful tool in unmasking genuine feelings. Practising vulnerability involves the courage to share one's true emotions, fears, and struggles with others. This openness fosters deeper connections and creates an atmosphere where authenticity is celebrated rather than concealed.

Mindful Emotional Regulation:
Mindful emotional regulation enables individuals to navigate and express their feelings intentionally. Rather than succumbing to impulsive reactions or suppressing emotions, practising mindfulness allows individuals to observe their emotions without judgement, fostering a more deliberate and authentic response.

Embracing Cultural Competence:
Understanding and embracing cultural competence is crucial for navigating the interplay between authentic emotional expression and cultural expectations. Individuals can engage in cross-cultural education, sensitivity training, or dialogue to foster an appreciation for diverse emotional norms and expressions.

Assertive Communication:
Adopting assertive communication is key to expressing genuine emotions effectively. Assertiveness involves clearly and respectfully communicating one's thoughts, feelings, and needs without aggression or passivity. This facilitates authentic expression while maintaining healthy interpersonal dynamics.

Engaging in Authentic Self-Reflection:
Authentic self-reflection is a continuous process of introspection and examination of one's values, beliefs, and emotions. Engaging in self-reflection allows individuals to identify and challenge emotional masks, fostering a deeper understanding of their authentic selves and promoting personal growth.

Setting Boundaries:
Setting boundaries is integral to emotional authenticity. Individuals can establish healthy boundaries that protect their genuine emotions and prevent the undue influence of external expectations. Clear boundaries empower individuals to express their true feelings while preserving their emotional well-being.

Seeking Professional Support:
In cases where emotional masking poses significant challenges, seeking professional support can be transformative. Therapists and counsellors provide a confidential and supportive space for individuals to explore and unmask hidden emotions, fostering emotional healing and growth.

Embracing Emotional Resilience:
Cultivating emotional resilience is essential in the pursuit of emotional authenticity. Embracing challenges as opportunities for growth, developing coping mechanisms, and learning from emotional experiences contribute to increased emotional resilience, allowing individuals to navigate the complexities of masked emotion with greater ease.

In conclusion, the journey toward emotional authenticity within the realm of masked emotion involves a combination of self-discovery, mindful practices, and intentional communication. These strategies empower individuals to unmask their true emotions, fostering a more genuine connection with themselves and others while navigating the intricate dance between societal expectations and authentic expression.

THE ENIGMA OF SOCIAL MASKS

SOCIAL MASKS IN DIFFERENT SETTINGS: AN INTRICATE TAPESTRY OF IDENTITY

In the intricate tapestry of human interaction, the enigma of social masks unravels across diverse settings, revealing a complex dance between authenticity and societal expectations. From professional landscapes to personal relationships, each setting presents a unique canvas for individuals to don masks tailored to navigate the intricacies of their social environments.

Professional Settings: Crafting Competence and Confidence

The Persona of Professionalism: In the realm of professional settings, individuals craft masks that project competence, confidence, and adherence to workplace norms. The professional mask becomes a tool for navigating hierarchies, fostering collaboration, and projecting a polished image that aligns with organisational expectations.

Emotional Regulation: The professional mask often involves a degree of emotional regulation. Individuals may suppress emotions such as stress or frustration to maintain composure, making emotional intelligence a valuable skill in navigating professional relationships. Striking a balance between authenticity and the demands of the workplace is crucial for fostering genuine connections.

Personal Relationships: Balancing Vulnerability and Connection

Intimacy and Vulnerability: Within personal relationships, social masks take on different hues, allowing individuals to express vulnerability, affection, and intimacy. However, societal expectations or past experiences may influence the adoption of masks that conceal true emotions to maintain harmony or avoid conflict. Navigating social masks in personal relationships involves a delicate balance between openness and the preservation of relational harmony.

Authentic Communication: The ability to communicate authentically within personal relationships is paramount. Open communication, trust, and a willingness to be vulnerable foster genuine connections. Unveiling the layers of social masks in personal settings allows for deeper emotional intimacy and understanding.

Social Gatherings and Events: Adapting to Social Atmospheres

Dynamic Social Masks: In social gatherings and events, individuals adopt social masks that align with the occasion. These masks may project sociability, enthusiasm, and adaptability to enhance collective enjoyment. The challenge lies in balancing the desire for authenticity with the social expectations of different events, allowing for enjoyable interactions without sacrificing genuine expression.

Navigating Social Dynamics: Social masks in these settings involve navigating the dynamics of group interactions. Individuals may tailor their expressions to contribute positively to the collective atmosphere, emphasising shared interests and fostering a sense of connection.

Cultural Contexts: Shaping Masks Through Cultural Lenses

Cultural Influences on Expression: Cultural contexts significantly shape the social masks individuals wear. Cultural norms dictate specific emotional displays deemed acceptable or inappropriate. Navigating social masks in diverse cultural settings requires cultural competence, an appreciation for differences, and an awareness of varying expectations regarding emotional expression.

Intersectionality of Identity: Social masks intersect with various aspects of identity, including race, ethnicity, sexuality, and socioeconomic background. Understanding the nuances of social masks within diverse and intersectional settings empowers individuals to navigate social dynamics with greater self-awareness, fostering a more authentic expression of their true selves.

Online and Virtual Spaces: Crafting Digital Personas

Digital Persona Crafting: In the digital age, social masks extend into online and virtual spaces. Individuals curate digital personas that present specific facets of their lives while concealing others. The anonymity of virtual spaces may encourage the adoption of masks that differ from one's offline identity.

Maintaining Online Authenticity: Navigating social masks in the digital realm involves maintaining authenticity while recognizing the impact of online interactions on mental well-being. Striking a balance between online and offline authenticity ensures a holistic expression of one's true self.

In conclusion, the enigma of social masks unfolds across various settings, weaving a complex narrative of identity, adaptation, and connection. Navigating this intricate tapestry requires a nuanced understanding of societal expectations, individual authenticity, and the diverse contexts in which individuals operate. Unravelling the enigma allows for a more authentic expression of the multifaceted self across the different landscapes of human interaction.

NAVIGATING PROFESSIONAL AND PERSONAL MASKS

In the intricate tapestry of human existence, individuals often find themselves navigating the dual realms of professional and personal life, each demanding a distinct set of social masks. let's explore the delicate balance between authenticity and societal expectations in these two interconnected spheres.

The Professional Mask: Crafting a Persona of Competence

Navigating Workplace Expectations: In professional settings, individuals craft a professional mask that projects competence, confidence, and adherence to workplace norms. This mask becomes a strategic tool for navigating organisational hierarchies, fostering collaboration, and projecting an image aligned with the demands of the professional landscape.

Emotional Regulation: The professional mask often involves emotional regulation. Individuals may suppress certain emotions, such as stress or frustration, to maintain a composed demeanour. Navigating the professional mask requires a keen understanding of emotional intelligence, allowing for authenticity within the boundaries of workplace expectations.

Striking a Balance: Balancing the professional mask involves navigating the thin line between authenticity and professionalism. Individuals must project a polished image while preserving their genuine selves. Striking this balance fosters positive workplace relationships and contributes to a healthy organisational culture.

The Personal Mask: Unveiling Authenticity in Relationships

Intimacy and Vulnerability: In personal relationships, individuals don a different mask that allows for expressions of vulnerability, affection, and intimacy. This mask aims to foster genuine connections with friends, family, and loved ones. Authenticity in personal relationships involves the courage to reveal one's true emotions and engage in open communication.

Maintaining Relational Harmony: Navigating the personal mask requires a nuanced approach to maintaining relational harmony. While it's essential to be authentic, individuals may also adapt their expressions to accommodate the needs and feelings of those they care about. This adaptive authenticity enhances understanding and strengthens personal connections.

Flexibility in Authenticity: Authenticity in personal relationships involves being flexible in one's expression of emotions. Individuals must navigate the ebb and flow of relationships, adapting their personal masks to the evolving dynamics while remaining true to their core values.

The Interplay: Juggling Professional and Personal Masks

Work-Life Integration: Juggling professional and personal masks requires a form of work-life integration. Integrating these masks involves bringing elements of authenticity into the professional realm and recognizing the impact of personal experiences on one's professional identity.

Strategic Adaptability: Strategic adaptability becomes crucial when navigating the interplay between professional and personal masks. Individuals must discern when to wear each mask, considering the context, social dynamics, and the specific demands of each realm. This strategic approach promotes authenticity without compromising professionalism or personal connections.

Challenges and Strategies: Navigating Dual Realms

Boundary Setting: Establishing clear boundaries between professional and personal life is essential. Setting boundaries allows individuals to compartmentalise their roles and navigate the distinct expectations of each realm without undue interference.

Self-Reflection: Engaging in regular self-reflection aids in navigating the dual realms. Understanding personal values, motivations, and aspirations allows individuals to align their masks with their authentic selves, promoting a sense of integrity across both professional and personal spheres.

Effective Communication: Effective communication is a cornerstone of navigating dual realms successfully. Transparent communication about personal needs, professional expectations, and the interplay between the two realms fosters understanding and cooperation with colleagues, superiors, and loved ones.

In conclusion, navigating the dual realms of professional and personal life involves the skillful adaptation of social masks while preserving authenticity. Striking the right balance empowers individuals to thrive in both spheres, fostering positive relationships, personal growth, and a harmonious integration of professional and personal identities.

THE INTERPLAY OF SOCIAL DYNAMICS

Within the enigma of social masks, the interplay of social dynamics adds layers of complexity to how individuals navigate group influences, conformity, and interpersonal relationships. This section explores the intricate dance of social dynamics within the context of the enigmatic social masks.

Navigating Group Influences in Social Masks:

Conforming within the Masked Collective: Social masks worn within groups are often influenced by collective norms. Individuals navigate the subtle pressure to conform to the group's expectations while still expressing their authentic selves within the confines of the mask.

Individuality Amidst Group Dynamics: The interplay of social dynamics involves striking a balance between conforming to group norms and preserving individuality. Individuals must navigate the tension between fitting into the collective mask and expressing their unique identity within the group setting.

Leadership Dynamics and Social Masks:

Leadership Roles and Masked Authority: In groups, leaders may wear a distinct social mask to project authority and guide the collective narrative. Navigating leadership dynamics within the enigma of social masks involves leaders balancing their authoritative masks while fostering a collaborative environment.

Followership and the Group Mask: Followers within the group navigate their roles by aligning with the group's masked direction. The interplay of social dynamics involves followers contributing to the collective mask while maintaining a sense of autonomy within their individual expressions.

Conflicts, Resolution, and Social Masks:

Masked Conflicts within Groups: Conflicts may arise when individual masks clash within the group dynamic. Navigating conflicts involves understanding the masked tensions, fostering open communication, and seeking resolutions that preserve the integrity of both individual and collective masks.

Mediation of Masked Disagreements: The interplay of social dynamics includes individuals playing roles as mediators or negotiators, helping resolve conflicts related to the enigma of social masks. Mediation requires a nuanced understanding of the masked perspectives and facilitating open communication for a harmonious resolution.

Cultural Considerations and the Masked Collective:

Diversity in Masked Expressions: Social masks within diverse groups are influenced by cultural considerations. Individuals navigate the masked expressions shaped by cultural backgrounds, fostering an inclusive environment that embraces diverse masked identities.

Cross-Cultural Communication with Masks: Effective communication within the enigma of social masks demands an understanding of cross-cultural differences. Navigating cross-cultural dynamics involves respecting and embracing masked expressions that may differ based on cultural nuances.

Influence, Change, and the Shifting Masked Landscape:

Social Influence and the Shifting Masked Landscape: The interplay of social dynamics involves the influence of masked individuals within the group. Navigating social influence includes understanding how masked expressions can shape the collective narrative and drive positive change.

Adaptation of Masks to Evolving Dynamics: As groups undergo changes, individuals adapt their masks to the shifting dynamics. Effective navigation within the enigma of social masks requires a collective understanding of how masked expressions may evolve over time.

In summary, the interplay of social dynamics within the enigma of social masks introduces a nuanced layer to group interactions. Navigating conformity, leadership dynamics, conflicts, cultural considerations, and the influence of masked expressions requires individuals to master the art of balancing collective expectations while preserving the authenticity of individual masked identities. This intricate dance contributes to the creation of a harmonious and dynamic masked collective.

UNMASKING DEFENCE MECHANISMS

COPING STRATEGIES AND DEFENCE MECHANISMS

Within the complex landscape of human psychology, individuals employ coping strategies and defence mechanisms as adaptive responses to life's challenges and stressors. This section explores the various ways individuals navigate adversity, manage stress, and protect their psychological well-being through coping strategies and defence mechanisms.

Understanding Coping Strategies:

Definition and Purpose: Coping strategies encompass conscious efforts individuals make to manage stress, adversity, or challenging situations. These strategies serve the purpose of maintaining emotional balance, reducing distress, and promoting resilience in the face of life's complexities.

Categorization of Coping Strategies: Coping strategies can be categorised into problem-focused coping, where individuals actively address the root causes of stress, and emotion-focused coping, where the focus is on managing emotional responses to stressors. Both types play crucial roles in adaptive functioning.

Common Coping Strategies:

Problem-Solving and Decision-Making: Individuals often employ problem-solving skills as a coping strategy, actively seeking solutions and making decisions to address the challenges they face. This strategy is particularly effective in situations where the stressor is within the individual's control.

Emotional Expression and Social Support: Coping can involve sharing emotions with others and seeking social support. Expressing feelings and receiving support from friends, family, or professionals can provide a valuable outlet for emotional release and problem sharing.

Mindfulness and Relaxation Techniques: Engaging in mindfulness practices and relaxation techniques, such as meditation or deep breathing, serves as a coping mechanism by promoting emotional regulation and reducing the physiological effects of stress.

Positive Reframing: Cognitive coping strategies involve reframing negative thoughts into more positive and constructive perspectives. By changing the interpretation of a situation, individuals can mitigate the impact of stressors on their mental well-being.

The Role of Defence Mechanisms:
Definition and Unconscious Nature: Defence mechanisms are unconscious psychological strategies individuals employ to protect themselves from uncomfortable emotions, thoughts, or realities. These mechanisms operate automatically and often serve to maintain psychological equilibrium.

Types of Defence Mechanisms: Defence mechanisms vary in complexity and function. Common examples include repression, where distressing thoughts are pushed into the unconscious, and projection, where individuals attribute their own undesirable traits to others.

Common Defence Mechanisms:

Denial: In denial, individuals refuse to accept the reality of a distressing situation. This defence mechanism provides temporary relief by shielding them from the emotional impact of the truth.

Regression: Under stress, individuals may revert to behaviours or reactions characteristic of an earlier developmental stage. This regression offers a retreat to a perceived safer and less stressful time.

Rationalisation: Rationalisation involves providing logical or reasonable explanations for behaviours or actions that may otherwise be emotionally challenging to accept. This defence mechanism allows individuals to justify their actions in a way that preserves their self-esteem.

Displacement: When unable to express emotions toward the source of stress, individuals may redirect their feelings toward a safer target. Displacement allows the release of pent-up emotions without directly confronting the initial stressor.

Healthy Coping and the Balance with Defence Mechanisms:

The Importance of Adaptive Coping: Healthy coping strategies involve adaptive responses that address the root causes of stress, promote emotional well-being, and contribute to personal growth. Problem-solving, seeking support, and engaging in self-care are examples of adaptive coping.

Awareness and Modification of Defence Mechanisms: Recognizing and understanding defence mechanisms is a crucial step toward personal growth and mental well-being. Individuals can work towards modifying maladaptive defence mechanisms through self-reflection, therapy, and conscious efforts to address underlying issues.

Combining Strategies for Resilience:

Integrated Approach: Resilience is often built through a combination of adaptive coping strategies and an awareness of defence mechanisms. By integrating problem-solving, emotional expression, and healthy defence mechanisms, individuals can navigate challenges with greater resilience and emotional balance.
In conclusion, coping strategies and defence mechanisms are integral aspects of human psychological functioning. Understanding the role of adaptive coping, recognizing defence mechanisms, and fostering a balanced approach contributes to emotional well-being and resilience in the face of life's complexities.

THE PSYCHOLOGY OF PROJECTION

Projection, a defence mechanism identified by psychoanalyst Sigmund Freud, is a fascinating psychological phenomenon where individuals unconsciously attribute their thoughts, feelings, or traits onto others. This section delves into the intricate workings of projection, exploring its mechanisms, manifestations, and psychological implications.

Understanding Projection:

Definition and Freudian Concept: Projection involves attributing one's unacceptable or unwanted thoughts, emotions, or traits onto others. It's a subconscious process where individuals disown certain aspects of themselves and see them manifested in external entities.

Mechanism of Projection: Individuals employ projection to avoid acknowledging or dealing with uncomfortable emotions or traits within themselves. By projecting these onto others, they distance themselves from acknowledging these aspects in their own personalities.

Manifestations of Projection:

Attribution of Negative Traits: One common manifestation involves attributing negative traits, emotions, or desires to others. For example, an individual feeling envy might project feelings of jealousy onto someone else, perceiving that person as envious instead.

Projection of Unacknowledged Desires: Unconscious desires or impulses that individuals find unacceptable in themselves may be projected onto others. This can manifest in situations where individuals accuse others of having motives or desires they're unwilling to admit to having.

Psychological Dynamics of Projection:

Ego Defense Mechanism: Projection serves as a defence mechanism, protecting the individual's ego from distressing or conflicting emotions. By projecting these onto others, individuals maintain a sense of moral superiority or emotional stability.

Unconscious Process: The process of projection occurs outside conscious awareness, making it challenging for individuals to recognize they are projecting their own traits or emotions onto others.

Examples of Projection in Everyday Life:

Interpersonal Conflicts: Projection can fuel conflicts when individuals project their own insecurities onto others. For instance, a person struggling with trust issues might accuse others of being untrustworthy.

Prejudices and Stereotyping: Societal prejudices can be rooted in projection. An individual projecting their fears or insecurities onto a particular group may develop prejudices or stereotypes about that group.

Addressing Projection:

Self-Reflection and Awareness: Recognizing projection requires introspection and self-awareness. Individuals can explore their reactions and emotions to uncover underlying feelings they may be projecting onto others.

Therapeutic Intervention: Therapy offers a supportive environment for individuals to explore and understand their unconscious processes, including projection. Therapeutic techniques can help individuals recognize and address projection tendencies.

Overcoming Projection and Personal Growth:

Integration and Acceptance: Overcoming projection involves integrating projected aspects back into one's self-awareness. Accepting and acknowledging these traits or emotions can lead to personal growth and emotional maturity.

Developing Empathy: Cultivating empathy and understanding toward oneself and others can diminish the need for projection. When individuals embrace their own complexities, they may become more tolerant and understanding of the complexities in others.

In conclusion, the psychology of projection unveils the intricate ways individuals navigate their unconscious desires, fears, and emotions. By recognizing and addressing projection tendencies, individuals can embark on a journey of self-discovery, fostering personal growth, and developing a deeper understanding of their own psyche and the complexities of human interactions.

BREAKING FREE FROM UNHEALTHY DEFENCES

Unhealthy defence mechanisms, while initially protective, can hinder personal growth and emotional well-being. This section explores strategies to identify, confront, and overcome these maladaptive defences, paving the way for healthier coping mechanisms and emotional resilience.

Recognition of Unhealthy Defence Mechanisms:

Identifying Maladaptive Patterns: Understanding and identifying maladaptive defence mechanisms is the first step toward breaking free from them. Common unhealthy defences include denial, projection, repression, and avoidance.

Self-Reflection and Awareness: Engaging in self-reflection and fostering self-awareness allows individuals to recognize patterns of behaviour or thought that indicate the use of unhealthy defences.

Understanding the Root Causes:

Exploring Underlying Triggers: Unhealthy defences often stem from past experiences, trauma, or unresolved conflicts. Identifying the root causes that trigger these defence mechanisms provides insight into their origins.

Therapeutic Exploration: Therapy offers a supportive environment to explore the underlying causes of maladaptive defences. Working with a therapist can help individuals gain deeper insights and develop strategies to address these root issues.

Embracing Vulnerability and Acceptance:

Courage to Be Vulnerable: Breaking free from unhealthy defences requires the courage to confront vulnerabilities and uncomfortable emotions. Embracing vulnerability allows for genuine self-expression and emotional growth.

Self-Acceptance: Accepting oneself with all vulnerabilities and imperfections fosters resilience and reduces the need for maladaptive defences. It involves embracing both strengths and areas for improvement.

Developing Healthy Coping Mechanisms:

Mindfulness and Emotional Awareness: Cultivating mindfulness practices enhances emotional awareness, allowing individuals to acknowledge and regulate their emotions effectively without resorting to maladaptive defences.

Effective Communication Skills: Learning healthy communication skills enables individuals to express emotions, needs, and boundaries assertively without relying on defence mechanisms such as avoidance or aggression.

Seeking Support and Connection:

Utilising Social Support Networks: Building and utilising supportive relationships can offer validation, empathy, and guidance. Seeking support from friends, family, or support groups aids in navigating challenging emotions.

Professional Assistance: Engaging with mental health professionals provides tools and techniques to address maladaptive defences. Therapists offer tailored strategies to overcome unhealthy patterns and promote healthier coping mechanisms.
Commitment to Personal Growth and Change:

Setting Personal Goals: Setting achievable goals for personal growth encourages individuals to actively work towards breaking free from maladaptive defences. Small steps lead to significant progress over time.

Embracing Change: Embracing change and being open to new perspectives and experiences fosters adaptability and resilience. Flexibility in thinking and behaviour enables individuals to develop healthier ways of coping.

In conclusion, breaking free from unhealthy defence mechanisms involves self-awareness, vulnerability, and a commitment to personal growth. By recognizing and addressing maladaptive patterns, embracing vulnerability, developing healthier coping mechanisms, seeking support, and being open to change, individuals pave the way for emotional resilience and authentic self-expression

THE INTERSECTION OF PERSONALITY AND MASKS

PERSONALITY TRAITS AND MASK ADAPTATIONS

This section explores the intricate relationship between personality traits and the adaptations individuals make in their behaviours, presenting different masks to navigate diverse social contexts. It delves into how various personality traits influence the adoption and adaptation of social masks.

Understanding Personality Traits:

Trait Theory: Personality traits refer to enduring patterns of thoughts, feelings, and behaviours that define an individual's characteristic way of interacting with the world. Traits encompass dimensions like extraversion, agreeableness, conscientiousness, neuroticism, and openness to experience.

Trait Continuum: Individuals possess a unique blend of these traits, which exist on a continuum. For instance, someone might lean toward being highly conscientious but moderately extraverted.

Personality Traits and Mask Adaptations:

Extraversion and Introversion: Extraverts may adapt masks that highlight sociability and outgoingness in social settings, while introverts might adopt masks that facilitate more reserved and reflective interactions.

Agreeableness and Conscientiousness: Agreeable individuals may wear masks that emphasise cooperation and harmony, while conscientious individuals might adopt masks focused on structure and reliability in their interactions.

Neuroticism and Emotional Stability: Those high in neuroticism might wear masks to mask their anxieties or insecurities, while individuals with emotional stability may adapt masks that project calmness and emotional control.

Openness to Experience: Those high in openness may adopt masks that demonstrate creativity and adaptability, while those lower in openness might prefer masks that adhere more closely to traditional norms.

Adaptive Masks and Social Contexts:

Professional Environments: In workplace settings, individuals with different personality traits may adapt masks that align with professional expectations. For example, a highly conscientious individual may emphasise their organised and detail-oriented traits.

Personal Relationships: Personality traits influence the masks individuals wear in personal relationships. A highly agreeable person might prioritise maintaining harmony, while someone with lower agreeableness might express their opinions more assertively.

Challenges of Mask Adaptation:

Authenticity Concerns: Adapting masks based on personality traits may lead to concerns about authenticity. Individuals might struggle with reconciling their true selves with the masks they wear in different contexts.

Stress and Strain: Continuously adapting masks according to personality traits can lead to stress and strain. For instance, introverts constantly adapting to more extraverted social environments may find it draining.

Embracing Authenticity within Masks:

Integration of Authenticity: Embracing authenticity involves integrating aspects of one's true self into the masks worn in different contexts. This alignment reduces the cognitive dissonance between the adapted masks and one's core identity.

Flexibility and Adaptability: Individuals can cultivate flexibility in their masks by adapting them based on the demands of a situation while staying true to their essential personality traits.

Self-Awareness and Personal Growth:

Enhancing Self-Awareness: Understanding one's personality traits and their influence on mask adaptations fosters self-awareness. It enables individuals to navigate social contexts more effectively while maintaining a sense of authenticity.

Personal Growth and Development: Striving for personal growth involves leveraging one's personality traits to develop adaptive masks that align with their values, fostering healthier and more authentic interactions across various contexts.

In conclusion, personality traits significantly influence the adaptations individuals make in their behaviours, shaping the masks they wear in different social contexts. By leveraging self-awareness, integrating authenticity into masks, and cultivating flexibility, individuals can navigate diverse social landscapes while staying true to their core identity and fostering personal growth.

INTROVERSION, EXTROVERSION, AND MASKING

This section delves into the nuanced relationship between introversion, extroversion, and the various masks individuals adopt to navigate social interactions. It explores how these personality traits influence the creation and adaptation of masks in different social contexts.

Understanding Introversion and Extroversion:

Introversion: Introverts tend to recharge by spending time alone, often preferring quieter and less stimulating environments. They may find social interactions draining and require solitude to rejuvenate.

Extroversion: Extroverts draw energy from social interactions and external stimuli. They often enjoy engaging with others, seeking social gatherings, and thriving in dynamic environments.

Mask Adaptation for Introverts:

Reserved Mask in Social Settings: Introverts may adapt masks that project a more reserved or contemplative demeanour in social contexts. This mask allows them to navigate interactions while preserving their need for solitude.

Strategic Social Engagement: Introverts might don a social mask strategically, engaging in social interactions for specific purposes or meaningful connections while ensuring they have time for solitude to recharge afterward.

Mask Adaptation for Extroverts:

Outgoing and Sociable Mask: Extroverts often wear masks that showcase their outgoing and sociable nature. These masks facilitate connections, lively conversations, and active engagement in various social settings.

Balancing Social Needs: Extroverts may adapt masks that balance their need for social interaction with occasional introspection. They might learn to moderate their extroverted tendencies in settings that require a more subdued approach.

Challenges and Benefits of Masking for Introverts and Extroverts:

Introverts: Struggles with Overexertion: Constantly adapting to a more extroverted mask may lead to overexertion for introverts, causing stress and exhaustion from prolonged social interactions.

Extroverts: Struggles with Solitude: Extroverts may encounter challenges in wearing a more introverted mask, finding extended periods of solitude challenging and potentially leading to feelings of isolation.

Benefits of Adaptation: Both introverts and extroverts can benefit from adapting their masks. Introverts may find increased social comfort, while extroverts may learn to appreciate solitude and introspection.

Embracing Authenticity within Mask Adaptation:

Integration of Authenticity: Both introverts and extroverts can aim to integrate authenticity into their adapted masks. This alignment fosters a sense of genuineness in social interactions while honouring their inherent traits.

Mindful Adaptation: Developing mindfulness helps individuals adapt their masks consciously, allowing introverts to engage in social interactions when needed and extroverts to appreciate moments of solitude without feeling isolated.

Leveraging Introversion and Extroversion for Effective Mask Adaptation:

Self-Awareness and Flexibility: Self-awareness enables individuals to recognize their natural tendencies and adapt masks that suit the demands of different social situations, fostering flexibility in their interactions.

Personal Growth and Balance: Both introversion and extroversion offer unique strengths. Embracing these traits leads to personal growth, allowing individuals to strike a balance between social engagement and personal recharge time.

In conclusion, the interplay between introversion, extroversion, and masking shapes how individuals navigate social interactions. By embracing authenticity, cultivating self-awareness, and leveraging the strengths of their natural tendencies, individuals can adapt masks that align with their personality traits, fostering healthier and more fulfilling social interactions.

THE INFLUENCE OF NEUROTICISM AND STABILITY IN MASK DYNAMICS

This section explores the impact of neuroticism and emotional stability on the masks individuals wear in social contexts. It delves into how these personality traits influence the creation, adaptation, and expression of masks in various interpersonal settings.

Understanding Neuroticism and Emotional Stability:

Neuroticism: Individuals high in neuroticism tend to experience negative emotions more intensely. They may exhibit tendencies toward anxiety, insecurity, and emotional volatility in response to stressors.

Emotional Stability: Conversely, emotional stability refers to individuals who maintain calmness, resilience, and a sense of control over their emotions even in challenging situations. They often display a more composed and steady demeanour.

Mask Adaptation for High Neuroticism:

Anxious or Defensive Masks: Individuals high in neuroticism might adapt masks that conceal their insecurities or anxieties in social situations. These masks may involve a defensive facade or an overly cautious approach.

Hyper Awareness of Social Responses: High neuroticism can lead to an intense focus on how others perceive them, influencing the masks they wear to project a specific image or to avoid potential judgement or criticism.

Mask Adaptation for Emotional Stability:

Composed and Resilient Masks: Those high in emotional stability might wear masks that project a composed, resilient, and calm demeanour in social interactions. These masks portray a sense of emotional control and balance.

Adaptive Response to Stress: Individuals with emotional stability may adapt masks that facilitate constructive responses to stressors. Their masks might reflect a sense of perspective and an ability to navigate challenges calmly.

Challenges and Benefits of Masking for Neuroticism and Stability:

Neuroticism: Struggles with Overthinking: Constantly adapting masks due to high neuroticism can lead to overthinking and excessive rumination about social interactions, contributing to heightened stress and anxiety.

Emotional Stability: Struggles with Suppression: Individuals with high emotional stability might struggle with suppressing emotions behind their masks, potentially hindering genuine emotional expression in social situations.

Benefits of Adaptation: Both neuroticism and emotional stability can benefit from adapting masks. Neurotic individuals might find a sense of reassurance, while emotionally stable individuals may reinforce their resilience.

Integrating Authenticity within Mask Adaptation:

Honest Expression of Emotions: Encouraging honest expression of emotions within adapted masks allows individuals to navigate social interactions authentically while acknowledging their emotional experiences.

Mindful Adaptation: Practising mindfulness assists individuals in consciously adapting their masks to suit various social contexts, helping neurotic individuals manage anxiety and emotional stability individuals maintain genuine emotional expression.

Leveraging Neuroticism and Emotional Stability for Effective Mask Adaptation:

Self-Awareness and Acceptance: Developing self-awareness around these traits allows individuals to accept their tendencies, fostering an understanding of how these traits influence their mask adaptations in social situations.

Balancing Vulnerability and Control: Neuroticism and emotional stability offer unique perspectives. Balancing vulnerability and control within adapted masks leads to personal growth, allowing individuals to express authenticity while managing their emotional experiences.

In conclusion, neuroticism and emotional stability significantly impact how individuals adapt masks in social interactions. By integrating authenticity, fostering self-awareness, and leveraging the strengths of these traits, individuals can navigate social contexts more effectively while embracing their inherent tendencies and promoting personal growth

CULTURAL DIMENSIONS OF MASKING

CULTURAL VARIATIONS IN PERSONA

This section explores the intricate relationship between culture and the personas individuals adopt. It delves into how cultural norms, values, and societal expectations shape the creation and adaptation of personas in diverse cultural contexts.

Understanding Cultural Influence:

Diverse Cultural Norms: Cultures vary significantly in their norms, traditions, communication styles, and social expectations. These differences profoundly influence how individuals present themselves in society.

Collectivism vs. Individualism: Cultures may lean towards collectivism, emphasising group harmony and interdependence, or individualism, valuing personal autonomy and self-expression. These orientations influence the masks individuals adopt.

Cultural Variations in Persona Creation:

Group Identity Emphasis: In collectivist cultures, individuals often prioritise group harmony, leading to masks that emphasise conformity and consideration for collective values. Masks might focus on preserving social harmony rather than individual traits.

Individual Expression Emphasis: Conversely, in individualistic cultures, masks may highlight individuality, personal achievements, and unique traits. There's often less emphasis on conforming to group norms, allowing for more diverse expressions.

Mask Adaptation in Different Cultural Contexts:

Communication Styles: Cultural variations in communication styles influence the adaptation of masks. High-context cultures might emphasise indirect communication, requiring subtle and context-dependent masks, while low-context cultures favour directness.

Hierarchy and Power Dynamics: Cultural attitudes towards hierarchy and authority shape masks. Some cultures value deference and respect to authority figures, resulting in masks that display deferential behaviour, while others encourage egalitarian interactions.

Challenges and Benefits of Cultural Persona Adaptation:

Challenges in Cultural Adaptation: Individuals navigating different cultural norms may face challenges in adapting their masks. Misinterpretation of cultural cues or mismatched expectations can lead to social discomfort or misunderstandings.

Benefits of Cultural Adaptation: Adapting masks according to cultural norms fosters social acceptance and smoother interactions within diverse cultural contexts. It promotes cross-cultural understanding and facilitates meaningful connections.

Embracing Authenticity in Cultural Persona Adaptation:

Cultural Sensitivity and Adaptation: Integrating cultural sensitivity into adapted masks allows individuals to navigate diverse contexts while respecting and adhering to cultural norms, fostering genuine connections.

Mindful Cross-Cultural Engagement: Practising mindfulness aids in adapting masks consciously, respecting cultural nuances, and allowing for an understanding of cultural expectations without losing authenticity.

Leveraging Cultural Diversity for Effective Persona Adaptation:

Cultural Awareness and Adaptability: Developing cultural awareness enables individuals to adapt masks that align with diverse cultural norms, fostering adaptability and successful social integration in varied cultural settings.

Balancing Cultural Expectations: Balancing adherence to cultural norms while maintaining personal authenticity within adapted masks leads to personal growth, fostering an appreciation for cultural diversity and enhancing social interactions.

In conclusion, cultural variations significantly influence how individuals create and adapt their personas. By integrating cultural sensitivity, fostering cultural awareness, and balancing adherence to cultural norms with personal authenticity, individuals navigate diverse cultural landscapes more effectively, fostering meaningful connections and cross-cultural understanding.

COLLECTIVE MASKS AND IDENTITY

This section explores the concept of collective masks, examining how individuals contribute to and are shaped by group identities. It delves into the dynamic interplay between individual and collective masks, shedding light on how shared identities influence personal expressions and shape the social landscape.

Understanding Collective Identity:

Definition: Collective identity refers to the sense of belonging and shared characteristics that individuals associate with a particular group. This can encompass various aspects, such as cultural, social, religious, or organisational affiliations.

Group Dynamics: Collective identity emerges through shared experiences, values, symbols, and narratives within a group. It provides a framework for individuals to connect with others who share similar attributes or affiliations.

Creation of Collective Masks:

Shared Norms and Values: Collective masks arise from shared norms and values within a group. They represent a collective facade that aligns with the identity and expectations of the group, fostering cohesion and a sense of belonging.

Symbolic Representations: Collective masks often incorporate symbolic representations that hold significance for the group. These symbols reinforce a shared narrative and serve as visual or behavioural markers of the collective identity.

The Interplay Between Individual and Collective Masks:

Personal Identity within the Collective: Individuals navigate a complex interplay between their personal identity and the collective identity of the group. This interaction influences the masks individuals wear, balancing personal expression with adherence to group norms.

Conforming and Differentiating: Individuals may conform to certain aspects of the collective mask to enhance a sense of belonging while simultaneously differentiating themselves by expressing unique traits within the boundaries of the collective identity.

Adaptation of Collective Masks in Different Contexts:

Social Contexts and Collective Masks: The adaptation of collective masks varies across different social contexts. In formal settings, individuals may emphasise professionalism, while in informal settings, the collective mask may relax to allow for more personal expressions.

Flexibility in Collective Masks: Collective masks exhibit flexibility as they adapt to the changing dynamics of the group and external influences. This adaptability ensures the sustainability and relevance of the collective identity over time.

Challenges and Benefits of Collective Masks:

Challenges in Individual Expression: Individuals may face challenges in fully expressing their individual identity within the constraints of the collective mask. Balancing personal authenticity with group conformity requires thoughtful navigation.

Benefits of Collective Identity: Collective masks contribute to a sense of belonging, shared purpose, and social cohesion. They provide a framework for individuals to connect with others, fostering a supportive environment within the group.

Embracing Individuality within Collective Identity:

Integration of Personal Traits: Embracing individuality within the collective identity involves integrating personal traits that contribute to the richness and diversity of the group. This integration fosters a dynamic and inclusive collective identity.

Celebrating Diversity: Recognizing and celebrating the diversity of individual expressions within the collective mask enhances the group's resilience and adaptability. It allows for a more comprehensive representation of the collective identity.

Leveraging Collective Identity for Social Impact:

Unity in Diversity: A strong collective identity that embraces individual expressions creates a powerful platform for social impact. It allows the group to unite under a shared purpose while leveraging the diversity of its members for innovative solutions.

Social Change and Advocacy: Collective masks can be leveraged for social change and advocacy. Groups with a strong collective identity often have a greater impact when advocating for shared values or challenging societal norms.

In conclusion, the concept of collective masks illustrates the intricate relationship between individual and group identity. By navigating the interplay between personal expressions and shared group norms, individuals contribute to the dynamic and evolving nature of collective identity, fostering a sense of belonging and creating opportunities for positive social impact.

NAVIGATING INTERCULTURAL MASKING

This section explores the complexities of intercultural masking, examining how individuals adapt their personas in cross-cultural interactions. It delves into the challenges, benefits, and strategies for navigating the nuances of diverse cultural contexts, shedding light on the dynamic interplay between personal identity and the expectations of different cultures.

Understanding Intercultural Masking:

Definition: Intercultural masking refers to the adaptation of one's persona in interactions with individuals from different cultural backgrounds. It involves adjusting communication styles, behaviours, and expressions to align with the expectations of diverse cultural contexts.

Cultural Awareness: Intercultural masking requires a heightened sense of cultural awareness, as individuals navigate the intricacies of social norms, communication styles, and values that differ across cultures.

Challenges in Intercultural Masking:

Mismatched Expectations: Individuals engaging in intercultural interactions may face challenges when their adapted masks do not align with the expectations of the other culture. Misinterpretation of cues or unfamiliarity with cultural nuances can lead to misunderstandings.

Authenticity Concerns: Balancing cultural expectations with authenticity poses a challenge. Individuals may feel torn between adhering to cultural norms and expressing their true selves, leading to a potential loss of personal authenticity.

Benefits of Intercultural Masking:

Enhanced Communication: Intercultural masking, when done thoughtfully, facilitates clearer and more effective communication. Adapting one's persona to align with the cultural expectations of the other party can foster mutual understanding.

Building Bridges: By adapting to the cultural norms of others, individuals can build bridges between diverse communities. Intercultural masking promotes inclusivity, respect, and a willingness to understand and appreciate different perspectives.

Strategies for Navigating Intercultural Masking:

Cultural Sensitivity Training: Engaging in cultural sensitivity training enhances individuals' understanding of diverse cultural norms, reducing the likelihood of cultural misunderstandings and promoting effective intercultural communication.

Active Listening: Actively listening to and observing cultural cues during interactions helps individuals adapt their masks more effectively. This fosters a deeper understanding of the other party's cultural expectations.

Flexibility and Open-Mindedness: Embracing flexibility and open-mindedness enables individuals to navigate intercultural interactions more successfully. Being receptive to different ways of expression and communication fosters positive engagement.

Embracing Authenticity in Intercultural Masking:

Balancing Authenticity and Adaptation: Striking a balance between authenticity and adaptation involves integrating one's true self while respecting and adhering to the cultural norms of the other party. This balance fosters genuine and meaningful intercultural connections.

Communication of Intent: Clearly communicating one's intentions and openness to adapting within the cultural context helps build trust. It signals a genuine willingness to engage authentically while respecting the cultural nuances at play.

Leveraging Intercultural Masking for Mutual Growth:

Cultural Exchange and Learning: Intercultural masking provides an opportunity for mutual learning and growth. By adapting and learning from different cultural perspectives, individuals contribute to a more inclusive and interconnected global community.

Promoting Cross-Cultural Understanding: Leveraging intercultural masking as a means to promote cross-cultural understanding contributes to the dismantling of stereotypes and biases. It fosters a more interconnected world where individuals appreciate and learn from diverse cultural expressions.

In conclusion, navigating intercultural masking involves a delicate balance between respecting cultural norms and expressing one's authentic self. By embracing cultural sensitivity, active listening, and a willingness to adapt while maintaining authenticity, individuals can navigate diverse cultural contexts, fostering meaningful connections and contributing to a more interconnected global society.

THE UNVEILING PROCESS

RECOGNIZING AND PEELING AWAY MASKS

This section delves into the process of recognizing, understanding, and gradually removing the masks individuals wear. It explores the importance of introspection, self-awareness, and vulnerability in unveiling one's true self while shedding societal and internalised personas.

Acknowledging Masked Behaviours:

Self-Reflection: Encouraging self-reflection allows individuals to identify the masks they wear in different situations. This involves recognizing patterns of behaviour, thoughts, and emotions that align with societal expectations rather than authentic self-expression.

External Feedback: Seeking feedback from trusted individuals can provide insights into how others perceive the masks one wears. External perspectives offer valuable information to recognize and acknowledge masked behaviours.

Understanding Masked Motivations:

Exploring Motivations: Examining the motivations behind wearing masks is crucial. It involves understanding the reasons behind adapting personas, whether for social acceptance, fear of judgement, or aligning with societal norms.

Uncovering Triggers: Identifying the triggers that prompt the use of masks allows individuals to pinpoint specific situations or environments where they tend to rely on these personas.

Embracing Vulnerability and Authenticity:

Courageous Self-Revelation: Embracing vulnerability involves the courage to reveal one's true thoughts, emotions, and values. It allows individuals to peel away layers of societal expectations to reveal their authentic selves.

Embracing Imperfections: Accepting imperfections and embracing authenticity fosters a deeper connection with oneself and others. It involves acknowledging that being genuine does not necessitate perfection.

Unveiling the True Self:

Gradual Unmasking: Peeling away masks is a gradual process. It involves consciously choosing authenticity over conformity in various aspects of life, allowing the true self to emerge over time.

Reconnecting with Core Values: Identifying and reconnecting with core values helps individuals align their actions and behaviours with their authentic selves. It serves as a compass guiding genuine self-expression.

Challenges in Unmasking:

Fear of Rejection: Fear of rejection or judgement can hinder the process of unmasking. Individuals may hesitate to reveal their true selves due to concerns about societal acceptance or potential criticism.

Unlearning Conditioned Behaviours: Overcoming ingrained societal conditioning requires effort and persistence. Unlearning habits formed by societal expectations and embracing authenticity can be challenging.

Cultivating Authentic Connections:

Authentic Relationships: Embracing authenticity fosters genuine connections with others who value and appreciate individuals for their true selves. Authentic relationships thrive on mutual understanding and acceptance.

Creating Safe Spaces: Establishing environments where individuals feel safe to express themselves authentically encourages the unmasking process. These spaces promote vulnerability without fear of judgement.

Embracing Growth and Self-Discovery:

Continuous Self-Discovery: The journey of unmasking is ongoing and intertwined with personal growth. Embracing this journey allows individuals to evolve and discover new facets of their authentic selves.

Celebrating Authenticity: Embracing authenticity as a source of strength rather than vulnerability allows individuals to celebrate their unique identities and contributes to a more authentic and diverse societal fabric.

In conclusion, recognizing and peeling away masks involves a journey of introspection, self-awareness, and courage to embrace vulnerability. By consciously choosing authenticity and gradually unveiling the true self, individuals embark on a transformative journey toward deeper self-acceptance and genuine connections with others.

SELF-DISCOVERY AND AUTHENTICITY

This section delves into the intricate process of self-discovery and the significance of authenticity in fostering a genuine sense of identity. It explores the journey of introspection, embracing uniqueness, and cultivating authenticity as a means of personal growth and fulfilment.

Embracing the Journey of Self-Discovery:

Inner Exploration: Self-discovery involves delving into one's beliefs, values, passions, strengths, and weaknesses. It's a journey of introspection, examining the layers that constitute one's identity.

Embracing Curiosity: Cultivating curiosity about oneself allows individuals to explore various aspects of their personality, preferences, and aspirations. It involves an open-minded approach to learning about oneself.

Unveiling Authenticity Through Self-Awareness:

Understanding Personal Narratives: Self-awareness involves understanding the narratives and stories individuals tell themselves about their experiences, shaping their perceptions and behaviours.

Recognizing Masked Behaviours: Being self-aware enables the recognition of behaviours and actions that align with societal expectations rather than one's true self. It empowers individuals to identify and acknowledge these masks.

Cultivating Authenticity:
Aligning with Core Values: Authenticity stems from aligning actions and decisions with one's core values. It involves making choices that resonate with personal beliefs and principles.

Expressing Vulnerability: Embracing vulnerability and expressing genuine emotions, thoughts, and beliefs fosters authenticity. It involves the courage to reveal one's true self without fear of judgement.

Embracing Uniqueness and Individuality:

Celebrating Uniqueness: Embracing individuality involves celebrating unique traits, quirks, and perspectives. It's about recognizing that authenticity lies in embracing one's distinct identity.

Honouring Personal Growth: Authenticity acknowledges personal growth and evolution. It involves embracing change and allowing oneself to evolve without compromising core values.

Overcoming Challenges in Authenticity:

Fear of Judgment: Fear of judgement or rejection can hinder authenticity. Overcoming this fear involves accepting that not everyone will resonate with one's authentic self, and that's acceptable.

External Expectations: External pressures and societal norms may conflict with personal authenticity. Overcoming this involves setting boundaries and staying true to oneself, even in the face of external expectations.

Authentic Living and Relationships:

Genuine Connections: Authenticity fosters genuine and meaningful relationships. It allows individuals to connect with others on a deeper level by sharing their true selves.

Healthy Boundaries: Authenticity involves setting and respecting personal boundaries. It allows for authentic connections while preserving one's emotional well-being.

Continual Growth and Self-Authenticity:

Continuous Self-Reflection: Self-discovery and authenticity are ongoing processes. Continual self-reflection fosters personal growth and deepens the understanding of oneself.

Evolution of Authenticity: Authenticity evolves as individuals grow and experience life. Embracing this evolution contributes to a more enriched and authentic life experience.

In conclusion, self-discovery and authenticity involve a journey of introspection, self-awareness, and embracing uniqueness. By cultivating authenticity, individuals embark on a path of personal growth, fostering genuine connections, and living a more fulfilled and enriched life.

NURTURING GENUINE CONNECTIONS

This section explores the significance of fostering authentic connections in personal relationships, highlighting the essence of vulnerability, empathy, and genuine communication in nurturing deep and meaningful connections.

Embracing Vulnerability in Relationships:.

Openness and Honesty: Genuine connections thrive on openness and honesty. Being vulnerable allows individuals to share their authentic selves, fostering deeper understanding and trust.

Mutual Sharing: Reciprocal vulnerability in relationships encourages mutual sharing of thoughts, emotions, and experiences. It creates a safe space for genuine interactions.

Cultivating Empathy and Understanding:

Empathetic Listening: Empathy forms the foundation of authentic connections. Listening with empathy and understanding allows individuals to connect on an emotional level, strengthening the bond.

Understanding Perspectives: Recognizing and respecting differing perspectives fosters empathy. It allows individuals to appreciate diverse viewpoints, nurturing a richer and more inclusive connection.

Genuine Communication and Expression:
Authentic Expression: Genuine connections are nurtured through authentic communication. Expressing thoughts, emotions, and needs sincerely strengthens the depth of relationships.

Active Engagement: Actively engaging in meaningful conversations, sharing experiences, and expressing genuine emotions encourages a deeper connection between individuals.

Building Trust and Respect:

Consistency and Reliability: Trust is fostered through consistent and reliable behaviour. Keeping commitments and being dependable reinforces trust in relationships.

Respectful Interaction: Respecting individual boundaries and values contributes to a nurturing environment for genuine connections. Respecting differences while celebrating similarities fosters respect in relationships.

Overcoming Barriers to Connection:

Overcoming Fear of Rejection: Fear of rejection may hinder genuine connections. Accepting vulnerability and understanding that not all connections will resonate aids in overcoming this fear.

Breaking Down Communication Barriers: Miscommunication and lack of genuine expression can hinder connections. Overcoming these barriers involves active listening, honest expression, and clarifying misunderstandings.

Deepening Emotional Intimacy:

Shared Emotional Space: Emotional intimacy is cultivated by creating a safe space for sharing emotions without judgement. It allows for a deeper understanding of each other's inner worlds.

Supporting Emotional Growth: Genuine connections provide support for emotional growth. Encouraging each other's personal development and being supportive enhances the relationship.

Continual Nurturing of Connections:

Investing Time and Effort: Genuine connections require ongoing investment. Regular communication, spending quality time together, and expressing appreciation nurture and sustain these connections.

Adapting to Changes: Relationships evolve over time. Adapting to changes while maintaining authenticity and open communication strengthens connections and allows for continued growth.

In conclusion, nurturing genuine connections involves vulnerability, empathy, and sincere communication. By fostering trust, respect, and emotional intimacy while overcoming barriers, individuals can cultivate deep and meaningful connections that enrich their lives and those of others.

BEYOND MASKS - A HOLISTIC APPROACH

INTEGRATING AUTHENTICITY INTO DAILY LIFE

This section focuses on practical strategies and actionable steps for seamlessly incorporating authenticity into the fabric of daily living. It explores the transformative power of aligning actions with personal values, fostering genuine connections, and creating a life that reflects one's true self.

Clarifying Core Values:

Reflective Exercise: Initiate the integration of authenticity by engaging in a reflective exercise to clarify and define core values. Identify the principles and beliefs that hold personal significance.

Daily Decisions: Ground daily decisions in these core values. Whether in relationships, work, or personal pursuits, consciously choose actions that resonate with these foundational principles.

Authentic Communication:

Open and Honest Dialogue: Foster authentic communication by prioritising openness and honesty. Share thoughts, feelings, and intentions transparently, both in personal relationships and professional interactions.

Active Listening: Authentic communication involves not only expressing oneself but also actively listening to others. Create space for genuine dialogue, valuing diverse perspectives, and fostering understanding.

Embracing Self-Expression:

Creative Outlets: Cultivate self-expression through creative outlets such as writing, art, or any form of personal expression. Engaging in creative activities provides a channel for authentic self-discovery.

Unapologetic Authenticity: Embrace unapologetic authenticity in personal expression. Let go of fears and inhibitions, allowing the true self to shine through without reservation.

Authentic Relationships:

Selective Connections: Surround yourself with relationships that encourage authenticity. Choose connections that value and support your true self, fostering an environment of mutual growth and understanding.

Vulnerability and Trust: Build trust in relationships through vulnerability. Share authentic experiences and emotions, creating a foundation for deeper and more meaningful connections.

Aligning Career with Passion:

Passion-Driven Choices: Integrate authenticity into professional life by aligning career choices with passions and values. Pursue work that resonates with your authentic self, enhancing job satisfaction and fulfilment.

Authentic Leadership: If in a leadership role, embody authentic leadership principles. Foster an environment where colleagues feel comfortable expressing their true selves, contributing to a positive and innovative workplace.

Mindful Living:

Present Moment Awareness: Practise mindfulness to cultivate present moment awareness. Being fully present in daily activities enhances the quality of experiences, promoting authenticity in actions.

Balancing Technology Use: Mindfully navigate technology use to avoid disconnection from authentic living. Create boundaries to ensure that online interactions complement, rather than replace, genuine face-to-face connections.

Overcoming Fear and Resilience:

Facing Fear Head-On: Address fears and insecurities directly, recognizing them as opportunities for growth. Confronting fears allows for the emergence of a resilient and authentic self.

Learning from Challenges: View challenges as learning opportunities. Embrace setbacks as part of the authentic journey, fostering resilience and strength in the face of adversity.

Creating Authentic Environments:

Personal Spaces Reflecting Identity: Curate personal spaces that reflect your identity and preferences. Surround yourself with elements that bring joy, comfort, and a sense of authenticity.

Nature and Authenticity: Connect with nature as a way to ground yourself in authenticity. Spend time outdoors, appreciating the simplicity and authenticity found in natural environments.

Teaching Authenticity to Others:

Lead by Example: Serve as an authentic role model by leading through example. Demonstrate the benefits and fulfilment derived from living authentically, inspiring others to embark on their own authentic journeys.

Encouraging Authenticity in Communities: Encourage authenticity within communities, whether familial, social, or professional. Foster an atmosphere where diverse voices are valued, and individuals feel empowered to express their true selves.

Reflection and Continuous Growth:

Regular Self-Reflection: Integrate regular self-reflection into your routine. Assess the alignment of actions with values, acknowledge personal growth, and identify areas for continued authenticity.

Embracing Evolution: Recognize that authenticity is a dynamic and evolving process. Embrace personal growth and changes, allowing authenticity to adapt and flourish with each stage of life.

In conclusion, integrating authenticity into daily life involves a deliberate and mindful approach to living in alignment with one's true self. By incorporating these practical strategies, individuals can create a life that reflects their core values, nurtures genuine connections, and fosters a sense of fulfilment and authenticity in every aspect of daily living.

TOOLS FOR SELF-REFLECTION

This section introduces practical tools and methods for cultivating self-reflection, an essential component of the journey towards authenticity. Utilising these tools empowers individuals to gain deeper insights into their values, beliefs, and behaviours, fostering personal growth and alignment with their authentic selves.

Journaling:

Daily Reflections: Incorporate journaling into your routine for daily reflections. Write about experiences, emotions, and observations, allowing thoughts to flow freely on paper. This practice encourages self-awareness and clarity.

Guided Prompts: Use guided journal prompts to focus your reflections. Questions such as "What are my core values?" or "What brings me joy?" can guide your introspection and prompt deeper self-discovery.

Mindfulness Meditation:

Present Moment Awareness: Practise mindfulness meditation to cultivate present moment awareness. This involves observing thoughts without judgement and bringing attention to the sensations of the present, fostering self-awareness.

Body Scan Meditation: Engage in body scan meditations to connect with physical sensations. This helps ground you in the present, fostering a deeper understanding of how emotions manifest in the body.

Personality Assessments:

Myers-Briggs Type Indicator (MBTI): Take personality assessments such as MBTI to gain insights into your personality preferences. Understanding your natural tendencies provides a framework for self-reflection on how you engage with the world.

StrengthsFinder: Identify your strengths using tools like StrengthsFinder. Recognizing and leveraging your strengths promotes self-awareness and empowers you to align your actions with your inherent abilities.

Values Assessment:
Values Clarification Exercises: Engage in values clarification exercises to identify and prioritise your core values. Understanding your values provides a foundation for decision-making and aligning your actions with what truly matters to you.

Values-Based Decision-Making: When faced with decisions, evaluate them against your core values. This ensures that your choices are in harmony with your authentic self, promoting a sense of fulfilment.

Feedback and 360-Degree Reviews:

Soliciting Feedback: Seek feedback from trusted friends, family, or colleagues. Their perspectives can provide valuable insights into how others perceive you, facilitating self-reflection on your impact on those around you.

360-Degree Reviews: In professional settings, participate in 360-degree reviews where feedback is gathered from various sources. This holistic view allows for a comprehensive self-reflection on your strengths and areas for growth.

Artistic Expression:

Visual Journals or Artwork: Express yourself through visual journals or artwork. Creative expression can serve as a powerful tool for self-reflection, allowing emotions and thoughts to be conveyed in a non-verbal form.

Photography or Collage: Create visual representations of your authentic self through photography or collage. Curate images that resonate with your identity, prompting contemplation on what elements truly define you.

Retreats and Solitude:

Personal Retreats: Schedule personal retreats to spend time in solitude. Retreats offer a dedicated space for self-reflection, allowing you to disconnect from daily distractions and connect with your inner thoughts.

Nature Walks or Hikes: Spend time in nature for quiet contemplation. Nature has a calming effect and provides an ideal backdrop for self-reflection, fostering a deeper connection with your authentic self.

Technology Detox:

Digital Sabbatical: Implement a digital detox by taking breaks from technology. Unplugging from constant connectivity creates space for introspection and reduces external influences on your thoughts and emotions.

Mindful Technology Use: When using technology, do so mindfully. Set intentional boundaries, such as designating specific times for emails and social media, to prevent digital overwhelm and promote self-reflection.

Group Reflection and Discussions:

Book Clubs or Discussion Groups: Join book clubs or discussion groups centred around personal development topics. Engaging in group reflections provides diverse perspectives and stimulates thought-provoking discussions.

Peer Mentorship: Establish peer mentorship relationships for mutual self-reflection. Sharing experiences and insights with others fosters a supportive environment for personal growth.

Regular Check-Ins:

Scheduled Self-Check-Ins: Designate regular times for self-check-ins. Reflect on your experiences, emotions, and goals, allowing you to monitor your progress in aligning your actions with your authentic self.

Goal Reviews: Periodically review your goals and aspirations. Assess whether these goals still align with your evolving sense of authenticity and make adjustments as needed to stay true to your values.

In conclusion, integrating these tools for self-reflection into your life provides a structured approach to understanding and aligning with your authentic self. By incorporating these practices into your routine, you embark on a transformative journey towards greater self-awareness, personal growth, and living in harmony with your true identity.

FOSTERING A CULTURE OF OPENNESS

This section explores the importance of cultivating a culture of openness in various contexts, from personal relationships to professional environments. Fostering an atmosphere of transparency and receptiveness encourages authentic communication, supports individual growth, and contributes to a more inclusive and harmonious community.

Creating Safe Spaces:

Emotional Safety: Cultivate emotional safety by ensuring that individuals feel secure expressing their thoughts and feelings without fear of judgement or reprisal. Establishing safe spaces allows for open dialogue and authentic self-expression.

Non-Judgmental Environment: Encourage a non-judgmental atmosphere where diverse perspectives are valued. A lack of judgement fosters openness and creates an environment where individuals feel free to share their authentic selves.

Promoting Transparent Communication:

Clear and Honest Communication: Advocate for clear and honest communication. Encourage individuals to express themselves transparently, fostering a culture where people feel heard and understood.

Addressing Misunderstandings Promptly: In situations where misunderstandings arise, promote addressing them promptly. Open communication prevents the escalation of conflicts and allows for the resolution of issues in a constructive manner.

Embracing Diversity and Inclusion:

Celebrating Differences: Foster a culture that celebrates diversity by acknowledging and appreciating individual differences. Embrace the richness that diverse perspectives bring to the community, promoting inclusivity.

Inclusive Practices: Implement inclusive practices that ensure all voices are heard and valued. Encourage collaboration and cooperation, recognizing that diverse backgrounds contribute to a more vibrant and dynamic community.

Encouraging Vulnerability:

Leadership Role Modelling: Leaders play a pivotal role in fostering openness. Lead by example, demonstrating vulnerability and authentic self-expression. This sets the tone for others to feel comfortable sharing their own vulnerabilities.

Acknowledging Imperfections: Cultivate a culture that acknowledges imperfections as part of the human experience. Encourage individuals to embrace vulnerability, recognizing that it is a strength that promotes authenticity.

Building Trust:

Consistency and Reliability: Foster trust through consistent and reliable behaviour. When individuals can depend on the reliability of their peers or colleagues, trust is strengthened, creating a foundation for open communication.

Confidentiality: Uphold confidentiality to build trust within the community. When individuals feel assured that their personal thoughts and experiences will be treated with respect and confidentiality, they are more likely to share openly.

Providing Constructive Feedback:

Constructive Feedback Culture: Establish a culture that values constructive feedback. Encourage individuals to provide feedback in a manner that is constructive, supporting personal and professional growth.

Receptivity to Feedback: Develop a receptivity to feedback within the community. Emphasise that feedback is a tool for improvement and self-reflection, not a form of criticism. Fostering a culture of openness includes being open to receiving constructive input.

Continuous Learning and Growth:

Promoting a Growth Mindset: Cultivate a growth mindset within the community. Embrace challenges as opportunities for learning and growth, fostering an environment where individuals feel supported in their personal development.

Learning from Mistakes: Encourage a culture that views mistakes as learning experiences. When individuals feel comfortable acknowledging and learning from their mistakes, it contributes to an open and adaptive community.

Team Building Activities:

Collaborative Projects: Initiate collaborative projects that require teamwork. Shared experiences in a collaborative setting promote bonding, communication, and a sense of unity within the community.

Team-Building Exercises: Organise team-building exercises that encourage open communication and trust-building. These activities contribute to a positive team dynamic and foster a culture of mutual support.

Training and Development Programs:

Communication Workshops: Conduct communication workshops that emphasise active listening, empathetic communication, and conflict resolution. Equip individuals with the skills necessary for effective and open communication.

Diversity and Inclusion Training: Implement diversity and inclusion training programs to raise awareness and foster a deeper understanding of diverse perspectives. Promote inclusivity through education and awareness.

Recognition and Appreciation:

Acknowledging Contributions: Foster a culture of openness by acknowledging and appreciating individual contributions. Recognizing the efforts of community members creates a positive atmosphere that encourages continued participation and openness.

Expressing Gratitude: Encourage the expression of gratitude within the community. Gratitude fosters a sense of connection and appreciation, contributing to a culture where individuals feel valued and motivated to share openly.

In conclusion, fostering a culture of openness involves intentional efforts to create a supportive and inclusive environment. By prioritising clear communication, embracing diversity, and promoting vulnerability, communities can cultivate a culture that values authenticity, encourages personal growth, and fosters a sense of belonging for all its members.

CONCLUSION: UNVEILING THE AUTHENTIC SELF

In the journey through the pages of "Beyond Masks: A Deep Dive into Personality Dynamics," we embarked on a profound exploration of the intricate layers that shroud our true selves. This book has been a guided odyssey, inviting readers to peel away the masks society encourages us to wear, uncovering the essence of our authentic identities.

From the conceptual realm of persona to the intricate exploration of the layers we hide behind, the narrative took us on a reflective expedition. We traversed the intricate landscapes of psychology, delving into the complex interplay between masks and the genuine self. The chapters unfolded as a tapestry, weaving together themes of self-discovery, vulnerability, and the courage to embrace authenticity.

"Beyond Masks" challenged us to confront the emotional and psychological intricacies of our lives, addressing the dichotomy between the roles we play and the individuals we truly are. The chapters on emotional expression and suppression, the impact of society on masks, and the unmasking of psychological patterns were beacons of illumination, guiding us through the labyrinth of our own minds.

The narrative evolved into an exploration of interpersonal dynamics, dissecting the nuances of social masks in different settings and unravelling the enigma of social masks. We navigated the delicate balance between personal and professional masks, delving into the interplay of social dynamics and the cultural variations that shape our personas.

As we reached the final chapters, the focus turned inward, guiding us through the intricate process of recognizing, peeling away, and embracing our authentic selves. Tools for self-reflection and fostering a culture of openness emerged as empowering guides on this transformative journey.

In the concluding chapter, "Integrating Authenticity into Daily Life," we found practical strategies to seamlessly weave authenticity into the fabric of our existence. The narrative celebrated the beauty of embracing imperfections, cultivating genuine connections, and living in alignment with our core values.

In the closing pages of "Beyond Masks," the invitation lingers—an invitation to continue the journey of self-discovery and authenticity. The conclusion is not a destination but a commencement, urging us to carry the wisdom gleaned from these pages into our daily lives. This book is not just a guide; it's an advocate for a more authentic, fulfilling existence—one unburdened by societal expectations, free from the constraints of masks, and brimming with the richness of genuine connection.

May "Beyond Masks" remain a companion in the ongoing quest for authenticity—a reminder that the true self is not a destination but a continuous unfolding, a beautiful dance of self-discovery and genuine expression. As we close this chapter, let us step into the world beyond masks, armed with insights, courage, and the profound understanding that authenticity is not only a choice but a celebration of our unique, unmasked selves.